Aleksandr Sergeevich Pushkin, George Henry Borrow

Targum

Or, metrical translations from thirty languages and dialects. And The talisman, from the Russian of Alexander Pushkin. With other pieces

Aleksandr Sergeevich Pushkin, George Henry Borrow

Targum

Or, metrical translations from thirty languages and dialects. And The talisman, from the Russian of Alexander Pushkin. With other pieces

ISBN/EAN: 9783337297480

Printed in Europe, USA, Canada, Australia, Japan

Cover: Foto ©Paul-Georg Meister /pixelio.de

More available books at **www.hansebooks.com**

TARGUM.

OR
METRICAL TRANSLATIONS
FROM THIRTY LANGUAGES
AND
DIALECTS.

BY

„The raven has ascended to the nest of the nightingale."
Persian Poem.

ST. PETERSBURG.
PRINTED BY SCHULZ AND BENEZE.
1835.

The following pieces, selections from a huge and undigested mass of translation, accumulated during several years devoted to philological pursuits, are with much diffidence offered to the public, the writer being fully aware that not unfrequently he has failed in giving his version that cast and turn, which constitute no slight part of the beauty of the original; a point the accomplishment of which the poetical Translator ought, in all instances, to bear particularly in view, but which he will invariably find the most difficult part of the task which he has undertaken; in comparison with which the rendering of the diction of his Author into tolerable verse is an easy achievement. Perhaps no person, amongst the many individuals who have distinguished themselves by skill in the targumannic art, has more successfully surmounted this difficulty than Fairfax, the Translator into English „octave rhyme" of „The Jerusalem," the master-piece of the greatest poet of modern Italy and, with one exception, of modern time.

— IV —

That the character of a nation is best distinguishable by the general tone of its poetry, has been frequently remarked, and is a truth which does not admit of controversy; the soft songs of the Persian, and the bold and warlike ditties of the Dane are emblems of the effeminacy of the one, and the reckless heroism of the other.—In most instances the writer in the selection of pieces for this little work has been guided by a desire of exhibiting what is most characteristic of the people to whose literature it belongs; At the same time, he has been careful that this desire should not lead him to the countenancing of any thing which could be considered as pregnant with injury to good taste and morals, and has in consequence been compelled to exclude from his anthology many a glorious flower, which he would gladly have woven therein, had he not been apprehensive that it was the offspring of a poisonous bulb. He cannot refrain from lamenting that in his literary researches he has too often found amongst the writings of those, most illustrious for their genius and imagination, the least of that which is calculated to meet the approbation of the Christian, or even of the mere Moralist; and in conclusion he will take the liberty of addressing to those who may feel within them the stirrings of a mind capable of mighty things, the sublime words, slightly modified, of an Arabian sage and poet: O man, though the years of thy worldly fame are destined to be equal in number to the doves of the heaven, they shall nevertheless have an end, but whatever thou shalt do or say, which is founded on the love of wisdom and of God, shall endure for ever.

Saint Petersburg.   June 1.   1835.

CONTENTS.

Ode to God.	From the Hebrew. ......
Prayer.	— — — Arabic. ......
Death.	— — — — — ......
Stanzas.	— — — — — ......
Odes.	— — — Persian. ......
Stanzas.	— — — Turkish. ......
Description of Paradise.	— — — — — ......
O Lord! I nothing crave but Thee.	— — — Tartar. ......
Mystical Poem.	— — — Tibetian. ......
Moral Metaphors.	— — — Chinese. ......
The Mountain-Chase.	— — — Mandchou. ...
The Glory of the Cossacks.	— — — Russian. ......
The Black Shawl.	— — — — — ....
Song.	— — — — — ......
The Cossack.	— — — Malo-Russian.
The Three Sons of Budrys.	— — — Polish. ......
The Banning of the Pest.	— — — Finnish. ......
Woinomoinen.	— — — — — ......
The Words of Beowulf.	— — — Anglo Saxon.
The Lay of Biarke.	— — — Ancient Norse
The Hail-Storm.	— — — — — —

The King and Crown.	From the Suabian. ...... p.	44
Ode to a Mountain Torrent.	— — — German.	45
Chloe.	— — — Dutch.	47
National Song.	— — — Danish.	49
Sir Sinclair.	— — — — —	51
Hvidfeld.	— — — — —	56
Birting.	— — — Ancient Danish.	59
Ingeborg's Lamentation.	— — — Swedish.	62
The Delights of Finn Mac Coul.	— — — Ancient Irish. ...	65
Carolan's Lament.	— — — Irish.	67
To Icolmcill.	— — — Gaelic.	68
The Dying Bard.	— — — — —	70
The Prophecy of Taliesin.	— — — Ancient British.	73
The History of Taliesin.	— — — — — — —	74
Epigram.	— — — Cambrian British.	77
The Invitation.	— — — — — — —	78
The Rising of Achilles.	— — — Greek.	82
The Meeting of Odysses and Achilles.	— — — — —	85
Hymn to Thetis and Neoptolemus.	— — — — —	90
The Grave of Demos.	— — — Modern Greek...	91
The Sorceries of Canidia.	— — — Latin.	92
The French Cavalier etc.	— — — Provençal.	97
Address to Sleep.	— — — Italian	98

The Moormen's March.	From the Spanish. …
The Forsaken.	— — — — — …
Stanzas.	— — — Portuguese.
My Eighteenth Year.	— — — French. …
Song.	— — — Rommany.

ERRATUM.

P. 14. L. 11. for „reverend" read „reverent."

ODE TO GOD.

From the Hebrew.

Reign'd the Universe's Master ere were earthly things begun;
When His mandate all created, Ruler was the name He won,
And alone He'll rule tremendous when all things are past and gone;
He no equal has nor consort, He the singular and lone
Has no end and no beginning, His the sceptre, might, and throne;
He's my God and living Saviour, rock to which in need I run;
He's my banner and my refuge, fount of weal when call'd upon;
In His hand I place my spirit at night-fall and rise of sun,
And therewith my body also; God's my God—I fear no one.

PRAYER.

From the Arabic.

O Thou who dost know what the heart fain would hide
Who ever art ready whate'er may betide;
Iu whom the distressed can hope in their woe;
Whose ears with the groans of the wretched are plied—
Still bid Thy good gifts from Thy treasury flow;
All good is assembled where Thou dost abide;
To Thee, save my poverty, nought can I show,
And of Thee all my poverty's wants are supplied;
What choice have I save to Thy portal to go?
If 'tis shut, to what other my steps can I guide?
'Fore whom as a suppliant low shall I bow,
If Thy bounty to me, Thy poor slave, is denied?
But oh: though rebellious full often I grow
Thy bounty and kindness are not the less wide.

DEATH.

From the Arabic.

Grim Death in his shroud swatheth mortals each hour,
Yet little we reck of what's hanging us o'er;
O would on the world that ye laid not such stress,
That its baubles ye lov'd not, so gaudy and poor;
O where are the friends we were wont to caress,
And where are the lov'd ones who dwelt on our floor?
They have drank of the goblet of death's bitterness,
And have gone to the deep, to return never more;
Their mansions bewail them in tears and distress;
Yet has paradise lovelier mansions in store;
Of the worth of the plume the dove strips from its dress
Were their views, save in memory heaven they bore.

STANZAS.

From the Arabic.

On a Fountain.

In the fount fell my tears, like rain,
And straight defil'd became its flood;
How should it undefil'd remain,
All purpled o'er with human blood?

The Pursued.

How wretched roams the weary wight,
Who rage of keen pursuers fears;
The whole earth's surface in his sight
A hunter's treacherous net appears.

ODES.

From the Persian.

1

Boy, hand my friends the cup, 'tis time of roses now;
Midst roses let us break each penitential vow;
With shout and antic bound we'll in the garden stray;
When nightingales are heard, we'll rove where roses blow;
Here in this open spot fill, fill, and quaff away;
Midst roses here we stand a troop with hearts that glow;
The rose our long-miss'd friend returns in full array;
No fairer pearls than friends and cups the roses know;
Poor Hafiz loves the rose, and down his soul would lay,
With joy, to win the dust its guardian's foot below.

2

If shedding lovers' blood thou deem'st a matter slight,
No goodness I can plead to scare thee and affright,
O Thou, in whose black locks night's Genius stands confest,
Whose maiden cheek displays the morning's Master bright.
My eyes to fountains turn, down pouring on my breast,
I sink amid their waves, to swim I have no might.
O ruby lip, by thee life's water is possest,
Thou couldst awake the dead to vigour and delight;

There's no salvation from the tresses which invest
Those temples, nor from eyes swift-flashing left and right.
Devotion, piety I plead not to arrest
My doom, no goodness crowns the passion-madden'd
    wight;
Thy prayer unmeaning cease, with which thou weariest,
O Hafiz, the most High at morning and at night.

8

O Thou, whose equal mind knows no vexation,
Who holding love in deep abomination,
On love's divan to loiter wilt not deign,
Thy wit doth merit every commendation.
Love's visions never will disturb his brain,
Who drinketh of the vine the sweet oblation;
And know, thou passion-smit, pale visag'd swain,
There's medicine to work thy restoration;
Ever in memory the receipt retain—
'Tis quaffing wine-cups to intoxication.

STANZAS.

From the Turkish of Fezouli.

O Fezouli, the hour is near,
Which bids thee from this world depart,
And leave—what now thou hold'st so dear—
The loves of thy too ardent heart.

Yet till that fated hour arrive,
Be thy emprises, every one,
If thou wouldst fain behold them thrive,
In God's Almighty name begun.

DESCRIPTION OF PARADISE.

From the Turkish.

(Translated from the metrical History of the World.)

Eight Gennets (†) there be, as some relate,
Or one subdivided, as others state;
The first Dar al Galal, the next is Salem,
And Gennet Amawi stands next to them;
Then Kholud and Nayim and Gennet Ferdous—
And that last as most lovely is pictur'd to us;
A seventh there is, Dar al Karar the same,
And an eighth there is also, and Ad is its name.
God made Dar al Galal of white pearls fair,
Then of rubies Al Salem, so red in their glare;
He made Gennet Kholud so splendid to stand
Of bright yellow corals, so smooth to the hand;
Then blest Gennet Nayim of silver ore—
Behold ye its strength, and its Maker adore.
Gold bricks He employ'd when He built Ferdous,
And of living sapphires Al Karar rose.
He made the eighth Gennet of jewels all,
With arbours replete 'tis a diamond hall.
Broad and vast is paradise-peak—
The lowest foundation is not weak.

(†) Gennet is a word of Arabic origin, and signifies paradise.

One over the other the stories are pil'd:
The loftiest story Ad is styl'd.
From above or below if you cast your eyes,
You can see the Gennets in order rise.
You ask, for whom are those mansions gay;
For the prophets of God, for his lov'd, I say.

Seven walls are plac'd, which to open are meant,
Far betwixt them is the extent;
Betwixt two walls the whole doth stand,
Walls uncrumbling, mighty and grand.
Within are bowers, cedar-woods dusk,
Houries and odours of amber and musk;
Eight are the gates for the eight estates,
Jewel-beset, gold-beaming gates;
Upon the first inscrib'd you see:
For those who repent this gate is free.
On the second: for those who up-offer pray'r;
On the third: for the sons of charity fair.
On the fourth this solemn inscription stands:
For those who fulfil the Lord's commands.
In painted letters the fifth doth say:
For those who for pilgrimage gold up-lay.
The sixth fair portal thus proclaims:
For ye who inhibit from sin your frames;
The seventh: for God's own warrior train,
Who bleed for his cause, nor flinch from pain.

'Tis written in white the eighth above :
For those who instruct for Allah's love (†).
For ye who serve God with heart and eye,
Control your passions when swelling high,
Your parents cherish and all your race,
For ye are the halls of joy and grace ;
For the prophets of God are they decreed,
Who His law in the sacred volumes read.

(†) No true Mussulman will receive any remuneration for communicating instruction.

O LORD! I NOTHING CRAVE BUT THEE.

From the Tartar.

O THOU, from whom all love doth flow,
Whom all the world doth reverence so,
Thou constitut'st each care I know;
   O Lord! I nothing crave but Thee.

O keep me from each sinful way;
Thou breathedst life within my clay,
I'll therefore serve Thee, night and day;
   O Lord! I nothing crave but Thee.

I ope my eyes and see Thy face,
On Thee my musings all I place,
I've left my parents, friends and race;
   O Lord! I nothing crave but Thee.

Take Thou my soul, my every thing,
My blood from out its vessels wring,
Thy slave am I, and Thou my King;
   O Lord! I nothing crave but Thee.

I speak—my tongue on Thee doth roam;
I list—the winds Thy title boom;
For in my soul has God His home;
   O Lord! I nothing crave but Thee.

The world the shallow worldling craves,
And greatness need ambitious knaves,
The lover of his maiden raves;
  O Lord! I nothing crave but Thee.

The student needs his bookish lore,
The bigot shrines, to pray before,
His pulpit needs the orator;
  O Lord! I nothing crave but Thee.

Though all the learning 'neath the skies
And th' houries all of paradise,
The Lord should place before my eyes,
  O Lord! I'd nothing crave but Thee.

When I through paradise shall stray,
Its houries and delights survey,
Full little gust awake will they,
  O Lord! I'll nothing crave but Thee.

For Hadgee Ahmed is my name,
My heart with love of God doth flame,
Here and above I'll bide the same;
  O Lord! I nothing crave but Thee.

MYSTICAL POEM.

Relating to the worship of the Great Foutsa or Buddh

From the Tibetian.

Should I Foutsa's force and glory,
Earth's protector, all unfold,
Through more years would last my story
Than has Ganges sands of gold.
Him the fitting reverence showing
For a minute's period e'en,
Bringeth blessing overflowing
Unto heaven and man, I ween.
If from race of man descended,
Or from that of dragon-sprite,
When thy prior course (†) is ended,
Thou in evil paths shouldst light,—
If Great Foutsa ever, ever
Thou but seek with mind sincere,
Thou the mists of sin shalt sever,
All shall lie before thee clear.
Whosoe'er his parents losing
From his early infancy,
Cannot guess with all his musing,

(†) Allusion is here made to metempsychosis or the transmigration of souls.

Where their place of birth might be;
He who sister dear nor brother,
Since the sun upon him shone,
And of kindred all the other
Shoots and branches ne'er has known
If of Foutsa Grand the figure
He shall shape and colour o'er,
Gaze upon it rapt and eager,
And with fitting rites adore,
And through twenty days shall utter
The dread name with reverend fear,
Foutsa huge of form shall flutter
Round about him and appear,
And to him the spot discover,
Birth-place of his flesh and bone (†);
And though evils whelm them over,
For his sake release them soon;
If that man unchang'd still keeping
From back-sliding shall refrain,
He, by Foutsa touch'd when sleeping,
Shall Biwangarit's title gain;
If to Bouddi's elevation,
He would win, and from the three
Confines dark of tribulation
Soar to light and liberty—

(†) His relations.

When a heart with kindness glowing
He within him shall descry,
To Grand Foutsa's image going,
Let him gaze attentively:
Soon his every wish acquiring
He shall triumph glad and fain,
And the shades of sin retiring
Never more his soul restrain.
Whosoever bent on speeding
To that distant shore, the home
Of the wise, shall take to reading
The all-wondrous Soudra tome;
If that study deep beginning,
No fit preparation made,
Scanty shall he find his winning,
Straight forgetting what he's read:
Whilst he in the dark subjection
Shall of shadowing sin remain,
Soudra's page of full perfection
How shall he in mind retain?
Unto him the earth who blesses,
Unto Foutsa, therefore he
Drink and incense, food and dresses
Should up-offer plenteously;
And the fountain's limpid liquor
Pour Grand Foutsa's face before,

Drain himself a cooling beaker
When a day and night are o'er;
Tune his heart to high devotion:
The five evil things eschew,
Lust and flesh and vinous potion,
And the words which are not true;
Living thing abstain from killing
For full twenty days and one,
And meanwhile with accents thrilling
Mighty Foutsa call upon —
Then of infinite dimension
Foutsa's form in dreams he'll see,
And if he with fixt attention,
When his sleep dissolv'd shall be,
Shall but list to Soudra's volume,
He, through thousand ages flight,
Shall of Soudra's doctrine solemn;
Ne'er forget one portion slight
Yes, a soul so richly gifted
Every child of man can find,
If to mighty Foutsa lifted
He but keep his heart and mind.
He who goods and cattle lacking
Is to fell disease a prey,
In whose household bones are cracking,
Cuts occurring every day,

Who though slumbering never resteth
From excess of bitter pain,
And what he in prayer requesteth
Never, never can obtain,—
To earth-favouring Foutsa's figure
If but reverence he shall pay
Dire misfortune's dreadful rigour
Flits for ever and for aye;
In his sleep no ills distress him,
And of nought he knows the want;
Cattle, corn and riches bless him,
Which the favouring demons grant.
Those, who sombre forests threading,
Those, who sailing ocean's plain,
Fain would wend their way undreading
Evil poisons, beasts and men,
Evil spirits, demons, javals (†),
And the force of evil winds,
And each ill, which he who travels
In his course so frequent finds—
Let them only take their station
'Fore the form of Foutsa Grand,
On it gaze with adoration,
Sacrifice with reverent hand—
And within the forest gloomy,
On the mountain or the vale,

(†) Goblins.

On the ocean wide and roomy
Them no evil shall assail.
Thou, who every secret knowest,
Foutsa, hear my heart-felt pray'r ;
Thou, who earth such favour showest,
How shall I thy praise declare ?
Through ten million calaps (†) hoary
If with cataract's voice I roar,
Yet of Foutsa's force and glory
I may not the sum out-pour
Whosoe'er the title learning
Of the earth's protector high,
Shall, whene'er his form discerning,
On it gaze with steadfast eye,
And at times shall offer dresses,
Offer fitting drink and food.
He ten thousand joys possesses,
And escapes each trouble rude.
Whoso into deed shall carry
Of the law each precept, he
Through all time alive shall tarry,
And from birth and death be free.
Foutsa, thou, who best of any
Know'st the truth of what I've told,
Spread the tale through regions, many
As the Ganges' sands of gold.

(†) Spaces of time.

MORAL METAPHORS.

From the Chinese.

1

From out the South the genial breezes sigh,
They shake the bramble branches to and fro,
Whose lovely green delights the gazer's eye—
A mother's thoughts are troubled even so.

From out the South the genial breezes move,
They shake the branches of the bramble-tree;
Unless the sons fair men and honest prove,
The virtuous mother will dishonor'd be.

The frigid fount with violence and spray
By Shiyoun's town upcasts its watery store;
Though full seven sons she give to life and day
The mother's heart is but disturb'd the more.

When sings the redbreast it is bliss to hear
The dulcet notes the little songster breeds;
But ah, more blissful to a mother's ear
The fair report of seven good children's deeds.

2

Survey, survey Gi Shoi's murmuring flood!
How its bamboos with living green are gay;
Survey the great, illustrious and good—
How sculptur'd, polish'd and refin'd are they!
What elegance and majesty they bear!
What witchery lurketh in their voice and eyes;
View them but once, and whilst thou breath'st the air
Thou'lt ne'er forget the great, the good and wise.

Survey, survey Gi Shoi's murmuring flood!
How its bamboos uptower in green array;
The bonnets of the great, the wise and good
At either ear an agate gem display;
Bright as a star the crownlet of their hair—
What witchery lurketh in their voice and eyes;
Survey them once, and whilst thou breath'st the air
Thou'lt ne'er forget the great, the good and wise.

Survey, survey Gi Shoi's murmuring flood!
Like to the green bamboos upon it's shore
Are the illustrious, the great and good—
More pure than gold, more soft than stannine ore;
The round imperial agate's not more sheen;
Ever magnanimous and constant found,
On glory's car they sit with placid mien,
And smile benign where jocund sports abound.

THE MOUNTAIN - CHASE.

From the Mandchou or Chinese Tartar.

(An extract from the „Description of Moukden" by the Emperor Kian Loung.)

Autumn has fled and winter left our bounds;
Now for the chase amongst the mountain grounds,
Our troops their implements and arms prepare.
Like colour'd rainbow see our banners glare;
While paler far and like the waning bow,
Rustle the standards in the winds that blow;
Piercing the mists, above our heads that lower,
Aloft behold our stately Toron (†) tower,
Flapping the skies with its embroider'd rim.
Away we journey, hale in mind and limb;
Our cars of state are creaking in the rear,
Whilst in the front the active guides appear.

And now our children mount their colts of speed,
Their sculptur'd cars full little here they need;
From the right side they take the arrow keen,
Ne'er to its quiver to return, I ween;
The bow, the left side's fitting ornament;
The bow, the tough and pliant bow is bent;

(†) The principal banner.

It yields a sound, like thunder from afar,
While flies the arrow, like a streaming star.

None now expects a tale of fabled might;
Wang Liyang's (†) bridle will no more delight;
Nor how his chariot Siyan Ou did guide;
Nor how, incas'd in hauberk's steely pride,
His hundred myriads, at the cymbals' sound,
The falcon launch'd, or slipp'd the eager hound;
Or giving rein to every fiery steed
No more precipitous Tai Shan would heed,
Than stair which leadeth to some upper bower;
Or swarming down tumultuous to the shore,
Chain'd the sea-waters with the nets they cast—
For such wild miracles the time is past.

Numerous and brilliant spreads our hunting train,
Stilly or noisily the aim is ta'en,
Forth the shaft speedeth all athirst for blood,
Whilst the string rattleth sharp against the wood;
The stags we scatter, in the plain which browse,
Or from his cavern the rough boar uprouse;
We scare the bokoin to the highest steeps,
Hunt down the hare, along the plain which leaps.
But though we slaughter, nor the work resign
When stiff and wearied are each hand and spine,

(†) Wang Liyang and Siyan Ou were ancient kings of China, and mighty hunters, of whose exploits many extravagant tales are related.

On field and mountain still the beasts are spied
Plenteous as grasses in the summer tide;
As at three points the fierce attack I ply,
Seeing what numbers still remain to die,
Captains, pick'd captains I with speed despatch,
Who by the tail the spotted leopard catch,
Crash to the brain the furious tiger's head,
Grapple the bear so powerful and dread,
The ancient sow, the desert's haunter, slay—
Whilst with applause their prowess we survey.

When thus fresh meat they have obtain'd with glee,
The largest beasts the hunters bear to me,
From which we separate and cast aside
Whatever beast by frontal wound has died;
To those the preference we at once decree,
In whose left side the fatal mark we see;
Those to be offer'd to our fathers' manes,
Within their high and consecrated fanes,
To dry and cure in wooden trays are laid,
Till bak'd or roast the offering is made.
Our guests they dine on the rejected prey,
And what they leave is safely stor'd away;
The gross amount of what is slain and shot
Falls to the carmen and the rabble's lot.

THE GLORY OF THE COSSACKS
An Ode.

From the Russian of Boris Fedorow.

Quiet Don!
Azure Don!
Who dost glide
Deep and wide,
To the proud
Cossack crowd
Drink which cheers,
Path which bears.

Quiet Don!
Azure Don!
Glory be
To thy sons,
Cossacks free
Warrior ones;
The world mute
Of their deeds
Hears the bruit—
Wide it speeds.

Light, I wot,
Hands they've not;

Down they fly
Thundringly,
Foes to crush,
E'en as rush
Down midst rocks
Eagle flocks.

Silent Don!
Azure Don!
Praise to their
Deeds so fair;
Fain our bright
Czar requite
Would each one,
Knew it might
Scarce be done—
Gave his son.

Silent Don!
Azure Don!
Sport and play,
Shine forth gay;
Gift most rare—
Alexander,
Russia's heir,
To thy clan
Given is for
Attaman.

Joys now every Cossack man,
Joys the Black sea's every stan (†)
    And Ural
    Flings its spray,
    Roars withal
    Night and day—
Joy to Cossacks—joy and glee
To each hero-regiment be:
    Given is an
    Attaman.

(†) Cossack village.

THE BLACK SHAWL.

From the Russian of Pushkin.

On the shawl, the black shawl with distraction I gaze,
And on my poor spirit keen agony preys.

When easy of faith, young and ardent was I,
I lov'd a fair Grecian with love the most high.

The damsel deceitful she flatter'd my flame,
But soon a dark cloud o'er my sunshine there came.

One day I'd invited of guests a gay crew,
Then to me there came creeping an infamous Jew.

,,With thy friends thou art feasting" he croaked in my
                                  ear—
,,Whilst to thee proves unfaithful Greshenka thy dear."

I gave to him gold and a curse, for his meed,
And I summon'd a thrall, ever faithful in need.

Forth rushing, I leap'd my tall courser upon,
And soft pity I bade from my bosom begone.

But scarcely the door of Greshenka I view'd
When my eyes became dark, and a swoon near ensu'd.

Alone to a far remote chamber I pac'd,
And there an Armenian my damsel embrac'd.

My sight it forsook me—forth flash'd my sword straight,
But I to prevent the knave's kiss was too late.

The vile, headless trunk I spurn'd fierce with my foot,
And I gaz'd on the pallid maid darkly and mute.

I remember her praying—her blood streaming wide—
There perish'd Greshenka, my sweet love there died.

The shawl, the black shawl from her shoulders I tore,
And in silence I wip'd from my sabre the gore.

My thrall, when the evening mists fell with their dew,
In the waves of the Dunau her fair body threw.

From that hour I have seen not her eyes' beamy lights,
From that hour I have known no delectable nights.

On the shawl, the black shawl with distraction I gaze,
And on my poor spirit keen agony preys.

SONG.

From the Russian of Pushkin.

Hoary man, hateful man!
Gash my frame, burn my frame;
Bold I am, scoff I can
At the sword, at the flame.

Thee as hell I abhor,
And despise heartily;
I another do adore,
And for love of him die.

Gash my frame, burn my frame!—
Nothing I will tell thee;
Man of age, man of rage,
Him thou'lt ne'er know from me.

Fresh as May and as gay,
Warm as Summer days he;
O how sweet, young and neat,
O how well he loves me.

O how him I carest
In the night still and fine;
O how then we did jest
At that grey head of thine.

THE COSSACK.

An ancient Ballad.

From the Malo-Russian.

O'er the field the snow is flying,
There a wounded Cossack's lying;
On a bush his head he's leaning,
And his eyes with grass is screening,
Meadow-grass so greenly shiny,
And with cloth the make of China;
Croaks the raven hoarsely o'er him,
Neighs his courser sad before him:
„Either, master, give me pay,
Or dismiss me on my way."
„Break thy bridle, O my courser,
Down the path amain be speeding,
Through the verdant forest leading;
Drink of two lakes on thy way,
Eat of mowings two the hay;
Rush the castle-portal under,
With thy hoof against it thunder,
Out shall come a Dame that moaneth,
Whom thy lord for mother owneth;
I will tell thee, my brave prancer,
When she speaks thee what to answer.

,, O thou steed, than lightning faster,
Tell me where's thy youthful master!
Him in fight thou hast forsaken,
Or has cast him down, I reckon."

,, Nor in fight I've him forsaken,
Nor have cast him down, I reckon,
The lone field with blood bedewing,
There the damsel Death he's wooing."

THE THREE SONS OF BUDRYS.

A Lithuanian Ballad.

From the Polish of Mickiewicz.

With his three mighty sons, tall as Ledwin's were once,
To the court-yard old Budrys advances;
,, Your best steeds forth lead ye, to saddle them speed ye,
And sharpen your swords and your lances.

For in Wilna I've vow'd, that three trumpeters loud
I'd despatch unto lands of like number,
To make Russ Olgierd vapour, and Pole Skirgiel caper,
And to rouse German Kiestut from slumber.

Hie away safe and sound, serve your dear native ground;
May the High Gods Litewskian defend ye!
Though at home I must tarry, my counsel forth carry:
Ye are three, and three ways ye must wend ye.

Unto Olgierd's Russ plain one of ye must amain,
To where Ilmen and Novogrod tower;
There are sables for plunder, veils work'd to a wonder,
And of coin have the merchants a power.

Let another essay to prince Kiestut his way,
To whose crosletted doys (†) bitter gruel!

(†) The knights of the German Order, who eventually christianized the pagan Lithuanians at the point of the lance and sword.

There is amber like gravel, cloth worthy to travel,
And priests deck'd in diamond and jewel.

Unto Pole Skirgiel's part let the third hero start,
There the dwellings but poorly are furnish'd;
So choose ye there rather, and bring to your father,
Keen sabres and bucklers high-burnish'd.

But bring home, above all, Laskian (†) girls to our hall
More sprightly than fawns in fine weather;
The hues of the morning their cheeks are adorning,
Their eyes are like stars of the ether.

Half a century ago, when my young blood did glow,
A wife from their region I bore me;
Death tore us asunder, yet ne'er I look yonder,
But memory straight brings her before me."

Now advis'd them he hath, so he blesseth their path,
And away they high-spirited rattle;
Grim winter comes chiding—of them there's no tiding;
Says Budrys: they've fallen in battle.

With an avalanche's might to the gate spurs a knight,
And beneath his wide mantle he's laden:

(†) Polish.

„Hast there Russian money—the roubles so bonny?"
„No, no! I've a Laskian maiden."

Like an avalanche in might riding comes an arm'd knight,
And beneath his wide mantle he's laden:
„From the German, brave fellow, bring'st amber so
    yellow?"
„No, no! here's a Laskian maiden."

Like an avalanche of snow the third up rideth now,
Nor has he, as it seemeth, been idle;
As the booty he showeth, old Budrys hallooeth
To bid guests for the brave triple bridal.

THE BANNING OF THE PEST.

From the Finnish.

The plague is solemnly conjured to leave the country, and the speaker offers to find a suitable conveyance, namely a demon-horse summoned from one of those mountains in Norway supposed to be inhabited by evil spirits and goblins.

Hie away, thou horrid monster!
Hie away, our country's ruin!
Hie thee from our plains and valleys!
I will find thee fit conveyance,
Find a horse for thee to ride on,
One whose feet nor slip nor stumble
On the ice or on the mountain;
Get thee gone, I do conjure thee;
Take thee from the hill a courser,
From the Goblin's Burg a stallion
For thy dreary homeward journey;
If thou ask me for conveyance,
If thou ask me for a courser,
I will raise thee one full quickly,
On whose back though mayest gallop
To thy home accurst in Norway,
To the flint-hard hill in Norway.
When the Goblin's Burg thou reachest
Burst with might its breast asunder;

Plunge thee past its sand-born witches
Down into the gulf eternal;
Never be thou seen or heard of
From that dismal gulf eternal.
Get thee gone, I do conjure thee,
Into Lapland's thickest forest,
To the North's extremest region;
Get thee gone, I do command thee,
To the North's most dusky region.

WOINOMOINEN.

From the Finnish.

Woinomoinen was, according to the Mythology of the ancient Finns, the second Godhead, being only inferior to Jumala. He was master of the musical art; and when he played upon his instrument produced much the same effect as the Grecian Orpheus, enticing fishes from the stream and the wild animals from the forest. The lines here translated are a fragment of a poem which describes a musical contest between Woinomoinen and the Giant Joukkawainen, in which the latter was signally defeated.

Then the ancient Woinomoinen,
On the bench himself he seated,
Took the harp betwixt his fingers,
On his knee about he turn'd it,
In his hand he fitly plac'd it.
Play'd the ancient Woinomoinen,
Universal joy awaking;
Like a concert was his playing;
There was nothing in the forest
On four nimble feet that runneth,
On four lengthy legs that stalketh,
But repair'd to hear the music,
When the ancient Woinomoinen,
When the Father joy awaken'd.
E'en at Woinomoinen's harping
'Gainst the hedge the bear up-bounded.

There was nothing in the forest
On two whirring pinions flying,
But with whirl-wind speed did hasten;
There was nothing in the ocean,
With six fins about that roweth,
Or with eight to move delighteth,
But repair'd to hear the music.
E'en the briny water's mother (†)
'Gainst the beach, breast-forward, cast her
On a little sand-hill rais'd her,
On her side with toil up-crawling.
E'en from Woinomoinen's eye-balls
Tears of heart-felt pleasure trickled,
Bigger than the whortle-berry,
Heavier than the eggs of plovers,
Down his broad and mighty bosom,
Knee-ward from his bosom flowing,
From his knee his feet bedewing;
And I've heard, his tears they trickled
Through the five wool-wefts of thickness,
Through his jackets eight of wadmal.

(†) The Mermaid.

THE WORDS OF BEOWULF, SON OF EGTHEOF.

From the Anglo Saxon.

Every one beneath the heaven
Should of death expect the day,
And let him, whilst life is given,
Bright with fame his name array.

For amongst the countless number
In the clay-cold grave at rest,
Lock'd in arms of iron slumber,
He most happy is and blest.

THE LAY OF BIARKE.

From the Ancient Norse.

The day in East is glowing,
The cock on high is crowing;
Upon the heath's brown heather
'Tis time our bands we gather.
Ye Chieftains disencumber
Your eyes of clogging slumber;
Ye mighty friends of Attil,
The far-renown'd in battle!

Thou Har, who grip'st thy foeman
Right hard, and Rolf the bowman,
And many, many others,
The forky lightning's brothers!
Wake—not for banquet-table!
Wake—not with maids to gabble!
But wake for rougher sporting,
For Hildur's (†) bloody courting.

Now food forego and drinking;
On war be ye all thinking,
To serve the king who've bound ye
For roof and raiment found ye;

(†) The war-goddess, according to the Northern Mythology

Reflect there's prize and booty
For all who do their duty;
Away with fear inglorious,
If ye would be victorious!

Great Rolf, the land who shielded,
And who its sceptre wielded,
Who freely fed and paid us,
With mail and swords array'd us,
Now lies on bier extended,
His life by treachery ended—
To us be like disaster,
Save we avenge our master.

THE HAIL-STORM.

From the Ancient Norse.

(This piece describes the disaster of Sigvald, Earl of Jomsborg, a celebrated viking or pirate, who, according to tradition, was repulsed from the coast of Norway by Hakon Jarl, with the assistance of Thorgerd, a female demon, to whom Hakon sacrificed his youngest son, Erling.)

For victory as we bounded,
I heard, with fear astounded,
The storm, of Thorgerd's waking,
From Northern vapours breaking.
Sent by the fiend in anger,
With din and stunning clangour,
To crush our might intended,
Gigantic hail descended.

A pound the smallest pebble
Did weigh, and others treble;
Full dreadful was the slaughter;
And blood ran out like water,
Ran, reeking, red and horrid
From batter'd cheek and forehead.
But though so rudely greeted,
No Jomsborg man retreated.

The fiend, so fierce and savage,
To work us further ravage,
Shot lightning from each finger,
Which sped, and did not linger;
Then sank our brave in numbers
To cold, eternal slumbers;
There lay the good and gallant,
Unmatch'd for warlike talent.

Our captain this perceiving,
The signal made for leaving,
And with his ship departed,
Down-cast and broken-hearted;
We spread our sails to follow,—
And soon the breezes hollow,
From shores we came to harry,
Our luckless remnant carry.

THE KING AND CROWN.

From the Suabian.

The King who well crown'd does govern the land,
And whose fair crown well fill'd does stand—
    That King adorns his crown, I trow;
And he who is thus by his crown adorn'd,
And for whose sake never that crown is scorn'd,
    Does bear a well-fill'd crown on his brow.

ODE

To a Mountain Torrent.

From the German of Stolberg.

O stripling immortal thou forth dost career
From thy deep rocky chasm; beheld has no eye
The mighty one's cradle, and heard has no ear
At his under-ground spring-head his infant-like cry.

How lovely art thou in the foam of thy brow,
And yet the warm blood in my bosom grows chill;
For awful art thou and terrific, I vow,
In the roar of the echoing forest and hill.

The pine-trees are shaken—they yield to thy shocks,
And crashing they tumble in wild disarray;
The rocks fly before thee—thou seizest the rocks,
And contemptuously whirlst them like pebbles away.

But why dost thou haste to the ocean's dark flood?
Say, art thou not blest in thine own native ground,
When in the lone mountain and black shady wood
Thou dost bellow, and all gives response to thy sound?

Then haste not, I pray thee, to yonder blue sea,
For there thou must crouch beneath tyranny's rod,
Whilst here thou art lonely, and lovely, and free—
Free as a cloud-bird, and strong as a God.

Forsooth it is pleasant, at eve or at noon,
To gaze on the sea and its far-winding bays,
When ting'd by the light of the wandering moon,
Or when red with the gold of the midsummer rays.

What of that? what of that? thou shouldst ever behold
That lustre as nought but a bait and a snare:
Ah, what is the summer sun's purple and gold
Unto him, who can breathe not in freedom the air?

O pause for a while in thy downward career!
But still art thou streaming, my words are in vain:
Bethink thee that oft-changing winds domineer
On the billowy breast of the time-serving main.

Then haste not, I pray thee, to yonder blue sea,
For there thou must crouch beneath tyranny's rod,
Whilst here thou art lonely, and lovely, and free—
Free as a cloud-bird, and strong as a God.

CHLOE.

From the Dutch of Johannes Bellamy.

O we have a sister on earthly dominions!
Cried two of the holy Angelical train,
And flew up to heaven with fluttering pinions,
But quickly to earth they descended again;
Their brothers, with voices triumphantly lifted,
Behind them came flocking this wonder to view,
More fast than the gleam from the cloud that is rifted,
Down, down to a forest of beeches they flew,

And there beheld Chloe, all rapt in devotion,
Upon the ground kneeling, unable to speak;
A tear-drop, the offspring of pious emotion,
Was streaming like dew down her beautiful cheek.
Confounded, astonish'd, in ecstacy gazing,
Around her the spirits aerial stood,
Then sudden their voices tumultuously raising
Cried: Father, we'll stay with her here in the wood!

Then frown'd the dread Father; his thunders appalling
To rattle began, and his whirlwinds to roar,
Then trembled the host, but they heeded his calling,
And Chloe up-snatching, to heaven they soar.

O we had a sister on earthly dominions!
They sang as through heaven triumphant they stray'd,
And bore with flush'd faces and fluttering pinions
To God's throne of brightness the yet praying maid.

NATIONAL SONG.

From the Danish of Evald.

Written to commemorate three great naval victories achieved by the three great Danish heroes, Christian, Juul, and Tordenskiold.

King Christian stood beside the mast
In smoke and mist.
His weapons, hammering hard and fast,
Through helms and brains of Gothmen pass'd,
Then sank each hostile sail and mast
In smoke and mist.
„Fly," said the foe, „fly all that can,
For who can Denmark's Christian
Resist?"

Niels Juul he mark'd the tempest's roar:
„Now, now's the tide!"
He hoists his banner, red as gore,
And plied his foemen aft and fore,
Loud crying 'midst the tempest's roar:
„Now, now's the tide!"
„Fly each, who knows a refuge path,
For who can Juul, when hot with wrath,
Abide!"

O North sea, Wessel's (†) flashes rent
Thy vapours dun.
Down to thy bosom heroes went,
For with those flashes death was blent;
From the fight rose a yell which rent
Thy vapours dun.
From Denmark lighteneth Tordenskiold,—
„Yield, yield to heaven's favourite bold,
And run."

Thou Danish path to fame and might,
Dark-rolling main!
Receive thy friend, who holds as light
The perils of the stormy fight,
Who braves like thee the tempest's might,
Dark-rolling main!
Bear me through battle, song and sport,
Until the grave, my final port,
I gain!

(†) Wessel was the family name of Tordenskiold. Tordenskiold is an epithet bestowed upon the Danish Admiral for his prowess and heroism. It signifies: shield of thunder.

SIR SINCLAIR. (†)

From the Danish of Edward Storm.

(At the commencement of the last century, Colonel Sinclair, a Scotsman in the service of the King of Sweden, landed upon the coast of Norway, at the time war was raging between the Danish and Swedish crowns, with a band of Scots which he had levied in his native country. After committing much havoc and cruelty, the invaders were destroyed to a man in a conflict with the peasantry, who had assembled in considerable number. Many of the broad-swords lost by the Scots in this encounter are to be seen in the Museum of Copenhagen, trophies of a victory achieved in a hallowed cause—the defence of the father-land against unprovoked aggression.)

Sir Sinclair sail'd from the Scottish ground,
To Norroway o'er he hasted;
On Guldbrand's rocks his grave he found,
Where his corse in its gore is wasted.

Sir Sinclair sail'd o'er the blue, blue wave,
For Swedish pay he hath sold him,
God help the Scot, for the Norsemen brave
Shall biting the grass behold him.

(†) This piece has already appeared in print, having been inserted some years since in the Foreign Quarterly Review, in an article on Danish poetry, of which the prose part proceeded from the pen of Doctor John Bowring.

The moon at night shed pale its light,
The billows are gently swelling;
See a mermaid merge from the briny surge,
To Sir Sinclair evil telling.

„Turn back, turn back, thou bonny Scot:
Thy purpose straight abandon:
To return will not be Sir Sinclair's lot,
Should Sir Sinclair Norroway land on."

„A curse on thy strain, thou imp of the main,
Who boding ill art ever!
For what thou dost preach, wert thou in my reach,
Thy limbs I would dissever."

He sail'd for a day, he sail'd for three,
With all his hired legions;
On the fourth day's morn Sir Sinclair he
Saw Norroway's rocky regions.

On Romsdale's sands he quickly lands,
Himself for a foe declaring;
Him follow'd then twelve hundred men
Such evil intentions bearing.

They vex'd the people, where'er they rov'd,
With pillage and conflagration;

Nor them old age's feebleness mov'd,
Nor the widow's lamentation.

The child was slain at the mother's breast,
Though it smil'd on the murderous savage:
But soon went tidings, east and west,
Of all this wo and ravage.

From neighbour to neighbour the message runs,
On the mountain blaz'd the beacon;
Into lurking-holes crept not the valley's sons,
As the Scots perchance might reckon.

,,The soldiers have follow'd the King to the war,
Ourselves must arm us, brothers!
And he who here his life will spare
Shall be damn'd as a cur by the others."

The peasants of Vaage, of Laxoe and Lom,
With axes sharp and heavy,
To the gathering at Bredaboig, one and all, come,
On the Scots fierce war to levy.

A pass, which all men Kringe call,
By the foot of the mountain goeth;
The Lauge, wherein the Scots shall fall,
Close, close beside it floweth.

The aged shooters are taking aim,
Each gun has been call'd into duty;
The Naik (†) his wet beard uplifts from the stream,
And with longing expects his booty.

Sir Sinclair fell the first, with a yell
His soul escap'd him for ever,
Each Scot loud cried when his leader died;
„May the Lord-God us deliver!"

„Now fierce on the dogs, ye jolly Norse-men,
To the chine strike down and cleave them!"
Then the Scots would fain be at home again,
Their vaunty spirits leave them.

Filling their craws to their hearts content
'Midst carnage the ravens wander'd;
The Scottish maids shall long lament
The young blood on the Kringe squander'd.

Not a single man escap'd, not one,
To his landsmen to tell the story;
'Tis a perilous thing to invade who wone
On Norroway's mountains hoary.

(†) The river-god.

A pillar still towers on that self-same spot,
Which Norraway's foes defyeth;
To the Norman wo, whose heart glows not
When he that pillar eyeth.

HVIDFELD.

From the Danish.

Our native land has ever teem'd
With warriors gallant-hearted,
Who bravery as their duty deem'd,
And ne'er from danger started;
Such Tordenskiold, and Adeler,
And Juul, and many others were.
Our native land has ever teem'd
With warriors gallant-hearted.

But who had e'er of bravery
The gallant Hvidfeld's measure?
Who e'er saw Death so plain as he,
And enter'd it with pleasure?
Ne'er shall his name oblivion meet,
For with his death he sav'd our fleet.
Our native land has ever teem'd
With warriors gallant-hearted.

'Gainst numerous foes we fought one day
A fight so fierce and gory,
And next the foe Sir Hvidfeld lay,
To danger close and glory;
And there was no man fought so stout
As Hvidfeld fought, that bloody bout.

Our native land has ever teem'd
With warriors gallant-hearted.

But as Sir Hvidfeld broadsides loud
Lay taking and returning,
His own fire set his vessel proud,
His Dannebrog, a burning.
,,Slip anchor, Sir," his sailors cry,
,,To land for safety let us fly!"
Our native land has ever teem'd
With warriors gallant-hearted.

,,No!" answer'd he, ,,for danger then
Midst Denmark's fleet we carry;
Shall it be risk'd by Danish men,
That they alive may tarry?
We'll die, but we'll avenge our death;
We'll fight until our latest breath."
Our native land has ever teem'd
With warriors gallant hearted.

,,Yes, to the latest breath we'll fight!"
His seamen answer'd, cheering;
Around was death in horrors dight,
But still they fought unfearing,
Till the fire reach'd the powder-store,
And all died heroes midst its roar.

Our native land has ever teem'd
With warriors gallant-hearted.

And Hvidfeld's fame shall ne'er decay,
His gallant seamens' never;
A worthy countryman shall they
In every Dane find ever;
When Denmark dear to us shall cry,
Like them will we grim death defy.
Our native ground shall still abound
With warriors gallant-hearted.

BIRTING.

A Fragment.

From the Ancient Danish.

It was late at evening tide,
Sinks the day-star in the wave,
When alone Orm Ungarswayne
Rode to seek his father's grave.

Late it was at evening hour,
When the steeds to streams are led;
Let me now, said Orm the young,
Wake my father from the dead.

It was bold Orm Ungarswayne
Stamp'd the hill with mighty foot:
Riv'n were wall and marble-stone,
Shook the mountain to its root.

It was bold Orm Ungarswayne
Struck the hill with such a might,
That it was a miracle,
That the hill fell not outright.

From the hill Orm's father cried,
Where so long, so long he'd lain;
„Cannot I in quiet lie
Deep within my dark domain?

Who upon my hill doth stand?
Who doth dare disturb my bones?
Cannot I in quiet lie
'Neath my heavy roof of stones?

Who doth dare my sleep to scare?
Who brings down this ruin all?
Let him fear, for now I swear
That by Birting he shall fall."

„I'm Orm Ungarswayne, thy son,
Youngest son, O father dear:
And to beg a mighty boon
In my need I seek thee here."

„If thou be Orm Ungarswayne,
Orm the kempion bold and free,
Silver, gold, last year I told—
All thou cravedst—o'er to thee."

„Thou wast free of gold and fee,
Glittering trash of little worth—

Birting now I crave of thee,
Birting bravest sword of earth."

,,Nèver shalt thou Birting win,
To obtain the King's fair daughter,
Till to Ireland thou hast been,
And aveng'd thy father's slaughter."

,,Give to me the Birting sword,
And with Birting bid me thrive,
Or I will thy sheltering hill
Into thousand atoms rive."

,,Stretch thou down thy right hand here,
Take the falchion from my side;
If thou break thy father's hill,
Dreadful wo will thee betide."

From the hill he Birting stretch'd,
Plac'd the hilt within his grasp:
,,Strong of hand and valiant stand,
That thy foes before thee gasp."

From the hill he Birting stretch'd,
Plac'd the hilt within his hold:
,,Save good fate on thee await,
I shall never be consol'd."

INGEBORG'S LAMENTATION

From the Swedish of Tegner.

(An extract from Frithiof's Saga.)

Autumn winds howl;
Ocean is swelling so stormy. — my soul,
Would with the sighs which I utter
Forth thou wouldst flutter!

Long did I view
Far in the West the sail which flew—
Happy my Frithiof to follow
O'er the wave hollow!

Blue billow run
O not so high, for it still sails on!
Stars, for my mariner sparkle,
As the nights darkle!

Spring will appear.
He will come home, but unmet by his dear
Or in the hall, or the dingle,
Or on the shingle.

She'll lie in mould,
All for her love's sake, pallid and cold,

Or she will bleed, by no other
Slain than her brother.

Hawk, left behind!
Thou shalt be mine and I'll prove ever kind:
Ever, wing'd hunter, I'll scatter
Food on thy platter.

Here on his hand
Work'd on my kerchief's hem thou shalt stand,
Pinions of silver and glowing
Gold-talons showing.

Hawk-pinions tried
Freia (†) one time, and around about hied;
Sought North and South to discover
Oder her lover.

E'en shouldst thou lend
Me thy brave wings, yet I could not ascend;
Only Death brings me, poor minion,
The divine pinion.

Hunter so free!
Sit on my shoulder and look to the sea;

(†) The Northern Venus.

Spite of our looking and yearning,
He's not returning.

When I'm at rest,
And he comes safe, do thou mind my behest
O with best greetings receive him,
Frithiof, who'll grieve him.

THE DELIGHTS OF FINN MAC COUL (†).

From the Ancient Irish.

Finn Mac Coul 'mongst his joys did number
To hark to the boom of the dusky hills;
By the wild cascade to be lull'd to slumber,
Which Cuan Na Seilg with its roaring fills.
He lov'd the noise when storms were blowing,
And billows with billows fought furiously,
Of Magh Maom's kine the ceaseless lowing,
And deep from the glen the calves' feeble cry;
The noise of the chase from Slieve Crott pealing,
The hum from the bushes Slieve Cua below,
The voice of the gull o'er the breakers wheeling,
The vulture's scream, over the sea flying slow;
The mariners' song from the distant haven,
The strain from the hill of the pack so free,
From Cnuic Nan Gall the croak of the raven,
The voice from Slieve Mis of the streamlets three;
Young Oscar's voice, to the chase proceeding,
The howl of the dogs, of the deer in quest;
But to recline where the cattle were feeding
That was the delight which pleas'd him best.

(†) The personage, who figures in the splendid forgeries of Mac Pherson under the name of Fingal.

Delighted was Oscar, the generous-hearted,
To listen when shields rang under the blow :
But nothing to him such delight imparted
As fighting with heroes and laying them low

CAROLAN'S LAMENT.

From the Irish.

The arts of Greece, Rome and of Eirin's fair earth,
If at my sole command they this moment were all,
I'd give, though I'm fully aware of their worth,
Could they back from the dead my lost Mary recall.

I'm distrest every noon, now I sit down alone,
And at morn, now with me she arises no more:
With no woman alive after Thee would I wive,
Could I flocks and herds gain and of gold a bright store.

Awhile in green Eirin so pleasant I dwelt,
With her nobles I drank to whom music was dear;
Then left to myself, O how mournful I felt
At the close of my life, with no partner to cheer:

My sole joy and my comfort wast thou 'neath the sun,
Dark gloom, now I'm reft of thee, filleth my mind;
I shall know no more happiness now thou art gone,
O my Mary, of wit and of manners refin'd.

TO ICOLMCILL.

From the Gaelic of Mac-Intyre.

On Icolmcill may blessings pour!
It is the island blest of yore;
Mull's sister-twin in the wild main,
Owning the sway of high Mac-Lean;
The sacred spot, whose fair renown
To many a distant land has flown,
And which receives in courteous way
All, all who thither chance to stray.

There in the grave are many a King
And duine-wassel (†) slumbering;
And bodies, once of giant strength,
Beneath the earth are stretch'd at length;
It is the fate of mortals all
To ashes fine and dust to fall;
I've hope in Christ, for sins who died,
He has their souls beatified.

Now full twelve hundred years, and more,
On dusky wing have flitted o'er,
Since that high morn when Columb grey
Its wall's foundation-stone did lay;

(†) The Gaelic word for nobleman.

Images still therein remain
And death-memorials carv'd with pain;
Of good hewn stone from top to base,
It shows to Time a dauntless face.

A man this day the pulpit fill'd,
Whose sermon brain and bosom thrill'd,
And all the listening crowd I heard
Praising the mouth which it proferr'd:
Since death has seiz'd on Columb Cill,
And Mull may not possess him still,
There's joy throughout its heathery lands,
In Columb's place that Dougal stands.

THE DYING BARD.

From the Gaelic.

O for to hear the hunter's tread
With his spear and his dogs the hills among;
In my aged cheek youth flushes red
When the noise of the chase arises strong.

Awakes in my bones the marrow whene'er
I hark to the distant shout and bay;
When peals in my ear; „We've kill'd the deer"
To the hill-tops boundeth my soul away;

I see the slug-hound tall and gaunt,
Which follow'd me, early and late, so true;
The hills, which it was my delight to haunt,
And the rocks, which rang to my loud halloo.

I see Scoir Eild by the side of the glen,
Where the cuckoo calleth so blithe in May,
And Gorval of pines, renown'd 'mongst men
For the elk and the roe which bound and play.

I see the cave, which receiv'd our feet
So kindly oft from the gloom of night,

Where the blazing tree with its genial heat
Within our bosoms awak'd delight.

On the flesh of the deer we fed our fill—
Our drink was the Treigh, our music its wave;
Though the ghost shriek'd shrill, and bellow'd the hill,
'Twas pleasant, I trow, in that lonely cave.

I see Benn Ard of form so fair,
Of a thousand hills the Monarch proud;
On his side the wild deer make their lair,
His head's the eternal couch of the cloud.

But vision of joy, and art thou flown?
Return for a moment's space, I pray,—
Thou dost not hear—ohone, ohone—
Hills of my love, farewell for aye.

Farewell ye youths, so bold and free,
And fare ye well, ye maids divine!
No more I can see ye—yours is the glee
Of the summer, the gloom of the winter mine.

At noon-tide carry me into the sun,
To the bank by the side of the wandering stream,
To rest the shamrock and daisy upon,
And then will return of my youth the dream.

Place ye by my side my harp and shell,
And the shield, my fathers in battle bore;
Ye halls, where Oisin and Daoul (†) dwell,
Unclose—for at eve I shall be no more.

(†) Ancient bards, to whose mansion, in the clouds, the speaker hopes that his spirit will be received.

THE PROPHECY (†) OF TALIESIN.

From the Ancient British.

Within my mind
I hold books confin'd,
Of Europa's land all the mighty lore;
O God of heaven high!
With how many a bitter sigh,
I my prophecy upon Troy's line (*) pour:

A serpent coiling,
And with fury boiling,
From Germany coming with arm'd wings spread,
Shall Britain fair subdue
From the Lochlin ocean blue,
To where Severn rolls in her spacious bed.

And British men
Shall be captives then
To strangers from Saxonia's strand;
From God they shall not swerve,
They their language shall preserve,
But except wild Wales, they shall lose their land.

(†) Written in the fifth century.

(*) The British, like many other nations, whose early history is involved in obscurity, claim a Trojan descent.

THE HISTORY OF TALIESIN.

From the Ancient British.

Talisson was a foundling, discovered in his infancy lying in a coracle, on a salmon-weir, in the domain of Elphin, a prince of North Wales, who became his patron. During his life he arrogated to himself a supernatural descent and understanding, and for at least a thousand years after his death he was regarded by the descendants of the ancient Britons in the character of a prophet or something more. The poems which he produced procured for him the title of „Bardic King;" they display much that is vigorous and original, but are disfigured by mysticism and extravagant metaphor; one of the most spirited of them is the following, which the Author calls his „Hanes" or history.

    The head Bard's place I hold
    To Elphin, Chieftain bold;
    The country of my birth
    Was the Cherubs' land of mirth;
    I from the prophet John
    The name of Merddin won;
    And now the Monarchs all
    Me Taliesin call.

    My inspiration's (†) flame
    From Cridwen's cauldron came;
    Nine months was I in gloom
    In Sorceress Cridwen's womb;

(†) Awen, or poetic genius, which he is said to have imbibed in his childhood, whilst employed in watching the cauldron of the sorceress Cridwen.

Though late a child—I'm now
The Bard of splendid brow (†);
When roar'd the deluge dark,
I with Noah trod the Ark.

By the sleeping man I stood
When the rib grew flesh and blood.
To Moses strength I gave
Through Jordan's holy wave;
The thrilling tongue was I
To Enoch and Elie;
I hung the cross upon,
Where died the ....

A chair of little rest
'Bove the Zodiac I prest,
Which doth ever, in a sphere,
Through three elements career;
I've sojourn'd in Gwynfryn,
In the halls of Cynfelyn;
To the King the harp I play'd,
Who Lochlyn's sceptre sway'd.

With the Israelites of yore
I endur'd a hunger sore;

(†) I was but a child, but am now Taliesin,—Taliesin signifies: brow of brightness.

In Africa I stray'd
Ere was Rome's foundation laid;
Now hither I have hied
With the race of Troy to bide;
In the firmament I've been
With Mary Magdalen.

I work'd as mason-lord
When Nimrod's pile up-soar'd;
I mark'd the dread rebound
When its ruins struck the ground;
When strode to victory on
The men of Macedon,
The bloody flag before
The heroic King I bore.

I saw the end with horror
Of Sodom and Gomorrah!
And with this very eye
Have seen the .... ;
I till the judgment day
Upon the earth shall stray:
None knows for certainty
Whether fish or flesh I be.

EPIGRAM.

On a Miser who had built a stately Mansion.

From the Cambrian British.

Of every pleasure is thy mansion void;
To ruin-heaps may soon its walls decline.
O heavens, that one poor fire's but employ'd,
One poor fire only for thy chimneys nine!

Towering white chimneys—kitchen cold and drear—
Chimneys of vanity and empty show—
Chimneys unwarm'd, unsoil'd throughout the year—
Fain would I heatless chimneys overthrow.

Plague on huge chimneys, say I, huge and neat,
Which ne'er one spark of genial warmth announce;
Ignite some straw, thou dealer in deceit—
Straw of starv'd growth—and make a fire for once!

The wretch a palace built, whereon to gaze,
And sighing, shivering there around to stray;
To give a penny would the niggard craze,
And worse than bane he hates the minstrel's lay.

THE INVITATION.

By Goronwy Owen.

From the Cambrian British.

(Sent from Northolt, in the year 1745, to William Parry, Deputy Comptroller of the Mint.)

Parry, of all my friends the best,
Thou who thy maker cherishest,
Thou who regard'st me so sincere,
And who to me art no less dear;
Kind friend, in London since thou art,
To love thee's not my wisest part;
This separation's hard to bear:
To love thee not far better were.

But wilt thou not from London town
Journey some day to Northolt down,
Song to obtain, O sweet reward,
And walk the garden of the Bard?—
But thy employ, the year throughout,
Is wandering the White Tower about,
Moulding and stamping coin with care,
The farthing small and shilling fair.
Let for a month thy Mint lie still,
Covetous be not, little Will;

Fly from the birth-place of the smoke,
Nor in that wicked city choke;
O come, though money's charms be strong,
And if thou come I'll give thee song,
A draught of water, hap what may,
Pure air to make thy spirits gay
And welcome from an honest heart,
That's free from every guileful art.
I'll promise—fain thy face I'd see—
Yet something more, sweet friend, to thee:
The poet's cwrw (†) thou shalt prove,
In talk with him the garden rove,
Where in each leaf thou shalt behold
The Almighty's wonders manifold;
And every flower, in verity,
Shall unto thee show visibly,
In every fibre of its frame,
His deep design, who made the same.—
A thousand flowers stand here around,
With glorious brightness some are crown'd:
How beauteous art thou, lily fair!
With thee no silver can compare:
I'll not forget thy dress outshone
The pomp of regal Solomon.

(†) Ale.

I write the friend, I love so well,
No sounding verse his heart to swell.
The fragile flowerets of the plain
Can rival human triumphs vain.
I liken to a floweret's fate
The fleeting joys of mortal state;
The flower so glorious seen to-day
To-morrow dying fades away;
An end has soon the flowery clan,
And soon arrives the end of man;
The fairest floweret, ever known,
Would fade when cheerful summer's flown.
Then hither haste, ere turns the wheel!
Old age doth on these flowers steal;
Though pass'd two-thirds of Autumn-time
Of summer temperature's the clime;
The garden shows no sickliness,
The weather old age vanquishes,
The leaves are greenly glorious still—
But friend! grow old they must and will.

The rose, at edge of winter now,
Doth fade with all its summer glow;
Old are become the roses all,
Decline to age we also shall;
And with this prayer I'll end my lay,

Amen, with me, O Parry say;
To us be rest from all annoy,
And a robust old age of joy;
May we, ere pangs of death we know,
Back to our native Mona go;
May pleasant days us there await,
United and inseparate!
And the dread hour, when God shall please
To bid our mutual journey cease,
May Christ, who reigns in heaven above,
Receive us to his breast of love!

THE RISING OF ACHILLES.

From the Iliad.

Straightway Achilles arose, the belov'd of Jove, round his shoulders
Brawny her Ægis spread, fair fring'd, his guardian Athena,
And his head with a cloud of golden hue and transparent
She has encircled about, whence darted fire resplendent.
As when fire from the town ascending clambers the ether
Out of the island afar, around which enemies gather—
Fierce the defenders all day engage in desperate warfare,
Forth from the town advanc'd; but soon as the sun has descended
Flame with beacons the dense, huge turrets; upwards the blazes
Flaring, struggling ascend to be seen by friends and by neighbours,
If with assistance in war o'er the sea in ships they are coming—
So from Achilles's head uptower'd the blazes to heaven;
Striding from out the wall, he stood o'er the trench, but he mingled
Not with the Greeks, for he heeded his mother's solemn injunction;

Standing, he shouted there, conjointly Pallas Athena
Scream'd, and trouble immense was caus'd thereby to the Trojans;
Like to the clamorous sound that's heard, when pealing the trumpet
Thrills through the city, besieg'd by bands of turbulent foemen,
E'en was the clamorous sound sent forth by Eacus' grandson—
Soon as the dreadful voice was heard of Eacus' grandson,
All their minds were amaz'd—the fair-man'd beautiful horses
Back'd with the chariots amain, such fear was awak'd in their bosoms;
Ghasted the charioteers survey'd the untameable blazes
Horribly round the brow of high, heroic Peleides
Burning, ignited by her the blue-eyed Goddess Athena
Thrice then o'er the deep trench loud shouted god-like Achilles,
Thrice were the Trojans confus'd and all their illustrious aiders;
Already round that trench had twice six champions fallen,
Spoil'd of their chariots and arms, so that gladly now the Achaians
Out of the tempest of darts the slain Patroclus dragging

Plac'd on the sorrowful couch; his comrades round it arrang'd them
Loudly lamenting, and thither there came swift-footed Achilles
Shedding the hottest of tears, when he saw his comrade so faithful
Stretch'd on that sorrowful couch, transfixt with the sharp pointed iron—
Him he had lately despatch'd with chariot and steeds to the war-field
Never, alas, to receive from that red war-field returning.

THE MEETING OF ODYSSES AND ACHILLES.

In Hades.

From the Odyssey.

Tow'rds me came the Shade of Peleidean Achilles,
And of Patroclus belov'd, and Antilochus daring and blameless,
And of Aias—of Him, who in bulk and beauty of figure
Far excell'd every Greek, to Peleides only inferior.
Me on the instant knew the Shade of Eacus' grandson,
And in sorrowful mood with words swift flowing address'd me.

Tell me Laertes' son, Odysses matchless in wisdom,
What fresh wondrous deed within thy brain thou art brooding,
That to the vasty deep of Hades down thou descendest,
Where the poor dead abide, mere idle shapes of the living.

Soon as the Hero ceas'd, in answer thus I address'd him:
Know, O Peleus' son, Achilles bravest of Grecians,
Seeking Tiresias hither I've come, to beg of him counsel
How I may Ithaca reach with its high-ridg'd, cloud-cover'd mountains;

Nor to Achaia I've been, nor my foot on the shore of my country
Wretch have I plac'd, whom ever misfortunes pursue; but no mortal
E'er was so blest, as Thou, or ever will be, O Achilles,
For when alive, as a God, we Argives held thee in honor;
Now e'en here, how high above the mighty departed
Thou dost in majesty rise; grieve not though dead, O Achilles.

Soon as these words I'd said, the Shade in answer address'd me:
Talk not of death to me, in mercy, glorious Odysses,
For on the Earth's green sod I'd rather toil as the hireling
Of some inglorious wight, and of one as poor as inglorious,
Than over all the dead in Hades reign as a Monarch;
But of my noble boy some tiding give me, I pray thee,
Whether or not he's fam'd as a gallant leader in battle;
And if aught thou hast heard of good old Peleus, tell me;
Still is he held in dread in Myrmidonian cities,
Or has he lost respect in Hellas-land and in Pthia,
Now old age has robb'd his hands and feet of their vigour?
Think not an aid so good I'm now in the light of the sun-beam,

As of old time I prov'd on the broad domain of the
                        Trojans,
When, in the Argives aid, I slew the best of their army;
Were I to enter now, as I am, the hall of my father,
Full little dread these hands would wake in the bosoms
                        of any,
Who in that hall do serve, and are kept by fear in
                        obeisance.

Soon as the Hero ceas'd, in answer thus I address'd him:
Nothing, alas, which regards the good, old Peleus know I;
But the whole tale of thy boy, thy Neoptolemus cherish'd,
I will with truth relate, by thee, great Shade, as com-
                        manded:
I myself had the luck in my own hollow ship to convey him
Forth from Scyros afar with a band of well-greav'd
                        Achaians.
Ever when round Troy's town in council grave we
                        assembled
He was the first to rise with a flow of eloquence faultless,
So that Nestor divine and myself confess'd him our
                        master;
But when on Troy's champain we strove with spear and
                        with buckler
Never amid the crowd you'd have found him or in the
                        phalanx—

Far in front he advanc'd, in courage shining the foremost,
And full many a man he slew in the rage of the combat;
There's no need to recount and to name in endless
successsion
All the renown'd he slew, whilst assisting strongly the
Argives;
Let it suffice that with steel he stretch'd Eurypilus
lifeless,
Telephos' hero-son, and around that hero were slaughter'd
All his Ceteian friends, ensnar'd by the smiles of the
damsels.

But when within the horse, the wondrous work of Epeius,
Enter'd the noble Greeks, with me their chosen commander,
Where we reclin'd thick and close, and one o'er the other
we panted,—
Then whilst the rest of the chiefs and princes high of the
Argives
Wip'd away feminine tears, and each shook in every
member,
Him in that hour of dread these orbs of vision beheld not
Either grow pallid or quake, or away from his cheek fresh
and downy
Wiping the tears—O no! and ever he begg'd for the
signal

Forth from the horse to emerge; and with ill intent to the Trojan,
Ever his spear he grip'd, or rattled the hilt of his falchion—
But when with ruin dread we raz'd the city of Priam
Fraught with the choicest prey the hero mounted his vessel,
Free from all scathe; his form nor smit from afar by the jav'lin,
Nor by the sword from near; no rare result of the combat,
For the tremendous Mars is no respecter of persons.

Scarce had I spoke when the Shade of Eacus' swift-footed grandson
Stalk'd with huge strides away o'er the flowery grass of the meadow,
Glad at the heart that its boy was fam'd 'mongst the brave as a warrior.

HYMN

To Thetis and Neoptolemus.

From the Greek of Heliodorus.

Of Thetis I sing with her locks of gold-shine,
The daughter of Nereus, lord of the brine,
To Peleus wedded, by Jove's high decree;
I sing her, the Venus so fair of the sea.
Of the spearman tremendous, the Mars of the fight,
Thunderbolt of old Greece, she was quickly made light,
Of Achilles divine, to whom Pyrrha an heir,
The boy Neoptolemus, gladly did bear,
The destroyer of Trojans, of Grecians the shield—
Thy protection to us, Neoptolemus yield!
Who blessed doth slumber in Pythia's green plain;
To accept this oblation of hymns from us deign,
And each peril drive far from our city benign.—
Of Thetis I sing with her locks of gold-shine.

THE GRAVE OF DEMOS.

From the Modern Greek.

Thus old Demos spoke, as sinking sought the sun the western wave:
Now, my brave lads, fetch us water, after supping let us lave;
O Lamprakes, O my nephew, down beside thy uncle sit—
When I'm gone, wear thou my trappings, and be captain, as is fit;
And do ye, my merry fellows, now my vacant sabre take,
And therewith green branches cutting, straight for me a pallet make;
Some one for the holy father, that I may confess me, run,
And that I to him may whisper all the crimes, in life I've done;
I've full thirty years as warrior, twenty five as robber pass'd;
Now I feel my end approaching, and I fain would breathe my last;
Me a tomb that's broad and lofty, O forget not to prepare,
For erect I'll stand within it, as in war, and weapons bear:
On the right side leave an opening, that the merry larks in spring,
Of its coming, welcome coming, may to me the tiding bring,
And for me in May's sweet season nightingales may sweetly sing.

THE SORCERIES OF CANIDIA.

From Horace.

(Canidia and other witches, having enticed a boy of high birth into some secret cell, proceed to bury him in the earth, up to the chin; in order that, when he has perished with hunger in that situation, his liver etc. may serve as ingredients for a draught, by administering which Canidia purposes to regain the affection of Varus, who has deserted her. The poem commences with the entreaties of the boy, and concludes with the imprecations which he utters when about to be abandoned to famine and inhumation.)

„Father of Gods, who rul'st the sky,
The earth and all the heavenly race!
What means this noise, why savagely
On me is turn'd each frightful face?—
By thy dear babes, if aid e'er lent
Lucine to thee in child-birth hour,
By this proud purple ornament,
By hands ne'er clasp'd to crave before,
I beg thee, Dame! thou wilt declare
Why she-wolf like thou me dost eye."
Stript of his tests of lineage fair
He stood, who rais'd this piteous cry—
A boy, of form which might have made
The Thracian furies' bosoms kind.
Canidia with her uncomb'd head
And hair with vipers short entwin'd,
Commands wild fig-trees, once that stood

By graves, and cypresses uptorn,
And toads foul eggs, imbued with blood,
And plume, by night-owl lately worn,
Herbs too, which Iolchos and Spain
Produce, renown'd for poisons dire,
And bone from hungry mastiff ta'en,
Straight to be burn'd in magic fire.
And now the witch strode through the house,
Hell-waters scattering wide around;
Her hair like hedgehog's bristling rose,
Or like the boar's whom hunters wound.
Veia, by pity unrestrain'd,
With pick-axe hastes the ground to tear,
And toil'd till sweat she panting rain'd,
That the poor wretch imburied there
Might slowly die, in sight of food
Renew'd each day, his head so far
Extant from earth, as from the flood
The heads of swimmers extant are;
That the parch'd marrow and the dry
Liver for a love-draught might be,
When fixt upon the feast the eye,
The craving eye should cease to see.
All Naples says in verity,
And all the neighbouring towns beside,
That Folia lewd of Rimini

Was present there, that dreadful tide—
She who with verse Thessalian sang
Down from their spheres the stars and moon.
Her uncut thumb with livid fang
The fell Canidia biting soon:
„Night and Diana," scream'd she out,
„Of my deeds faithful witnesses!
Ye who spread silence wide about,
When wrought are sacred mysteries!
Now aid me: in my foe's house bid
Your wrath and power divine to hie,
Whilst in their awful forests hid,
O'ercome with sleep, the wild beasts lie:
May suburb curs, that all may jeer,
Bay the old lecher, smear'd with nard (†),
More choice than which these fingers ne'er
Have, skilful, at my need prepar'd.
But why have charms by me employ'd,
Less luck than her's, Medea dread,
With which her rival she destroy'd,
Great Creon's child, then proudly fled,
When the robe bane-imbued, her gift,
Enwrapp'd the new-wed bride in flame?

(†) They had, it seems, made an image of Varus, and besmeared it with some high-smelling ointment, in the hope that Varus, by sympathy, would bear about him the odour of the same, so that the dogs might bay at him in his nocturnal excursions.

But neither herb, nor root from rift
Of lone rock ta'en, are here to blame;
In every harlot's bed lies he
Anointed with oblivion;
Ah, ah, 'tis plain he walketh free
Protected by some mightier one.
But Varus! thou shalt suffer yet!
Thou shalt re-seek these longing arms,
And ne'er from me re-alienate
Thy mind, enthrall'd by Marsan charms.
A cup more powerful I for thee
Will soon prepare, disdainful wretch!
Ere shall the sky sink 'neath the sea,
And that shall o'er the earth out-stretch,
Than with my love thou shalt not burn,
Like pitch, which in these flames I throw."
Not with mild words their bosoms stern
To melt, as erst, the boy sought now;
But madly reckless he began
The direst curses forth to rave:
„And do not think your sorceries can
Yourselves from retribution save:
Your curse I'll prove; my deathless hate
By sacrifice ne'er sooth'd shall be;
But when I perish, bid by fate,
A night-ghost ye shall have in me.

With crook'd nails I'll your faces tear,
For great is injur'd spirits might,
On your breasts seated, hard I'll bear,
And banish sleep with ceaseless fright;
Ye through the streets with stones the crowd
To death shall pelt, ye hags obscene!
Your limbs, no sepulture allow'd,
The wolves shall tear and birds unclean.
My parents who, though grey and old,
Shall me survive, their youthful boy
When they that spectacle behold
Shall clap their hands and smile for joy."

THE FRENCH CAVALIER, ETC.

From the Provençal.

The French cavalier shall have my praise,
And the dame of the Catalan;
Of the Genoese the honorable ways,
And a court on Castilian plan;
The gentle, gentle Provençal lays,
The dance of Trevisan;
The heart which the Aragonese displays,
And the pearl of Julian;
The hands and face of the English race,
And a youth of Tuscan clan.

ADDRESS TO SLEEP.

From the Italian of Vincenzio Filicaia.

Sweet death of sense, oblivion of ill,
Sleep! who from war, from time to time, dost bear
Poor, wretched mortals, and in peace dost still—
Compose the discords, which my bosom tear,
For a brief space, and kindly interpose
Thy soothing wings betwixt me and my care.
These eyes, which seem in love with weeping, close!
And make my senses for a time thy bower,
That whilst I sleep I may my sorrows lose.
I do not crave that thou the wand of power,
Three times in Lethe dipp'd, at me shouldst shake,
And all my senses sprinkle o'er and o'er;
Let souls, more fortunate, thereof partake—
Of languid rest a portion scant and slight,
My weary, wandering eyes content will make.
Now all the world is hush'd; to sleep invite
The falling stars, and lull'd appears the main,
And prone the winds have slumber'd on their flight;
I, I alone—who will believe my strain?
I, I alone, in this repose profound
And universal, no repose can gain;
Four suns, and moons as many, have come round,

Since tasted last these wretched lights of mine
Of thee, sweet cordial to the sick and sound.
There on the rough peaks of the Apennine,
Or where to Arno's breast in dower doth throw
The Pesa limpid waves and crystalline—
With eye-balls motionless, and hearts which glow
With zeal and faith, repel thee as a sin,
Perchance some band of eremites e'en now;
O come from thence! and for one hour within
My bosom deign to tarry, then retreat,
And in some other breast admission win;
I call thee thence! but if thou'dst hither fleet
From where now Love excludes thy gentle might—
Love with its phantasies so bitter sweet,—
Avaunt, avaunt! full wretched is my plight!
But honor, virtue I adore 'bove all,
Nor to profane night's sacred hours delight,
Descend on me, as on some mountain tall
Descends the snow, and there, dissolving soon,
Back to its pristine element doth fall;
Or that same dew, which suckleth bland and boon
Each green grass blade when morn begins to peep,
That none neglected may its faith impugn.
Before I die thy humid pinions sweep
Above me once, but O to stain forbear
The heart which still immaculate I keep!

But thou com'st not, and now, with rosy hair
From Ganges hastening, to all things again
Their native hue restores Day's harbinger.
Perhaps thou'st come, and ah, my cruel pain
And wakeful thoughts thee ingress have denied
Into my eyes, or hurl'd thee out amain.
Since, blundering archer, thou dost shoot aside,
Or snapp'st thy every dart my breast upon,
To me thy wand be never more applied!
Away, away! grim Death can blunt alone
My miseries' point, and ne'er till life be spent
I shall the hour of dear repose have won.
O how the strife within is vehement!
Now reason wins, now madness holds the sway;
So much my ill can do, nor I prevent.
O may this soul of mine from out its clay
Fly to repose elsewhere! I'm sure to see
My last hour once; and though far, far away
The feign'd death keep, the true shall visit me.

THE MOORMEN'S MARCH FROM GRANADA.

An Ancient Ballad.

From the Spanish.

„Reduan, I but lately heard
From thy mouth the sounding word,
That for me the town of Jaen
In one night thou wouldst obtain;
Reduan, if thou do the same,
Double pay thou mayest claim;
Save thy word perform'd I see,
From Granada thou shalt flee,
Banish'd to a far frontier,
Where thy lady shall not cheer."
Reduan, at the Monarch's side,
With unalter'd mien replied:
„Though the word I never said,
It I'll do, or lose my head."
Reduan crav'd one thousand men—
Five the Monarch gave him then.
From Elvira's portal-arch
See the cavalcado march:
Many a Moor of birth was there,
Many a bay, high-blooded mare,

Many a lance in fist of might,
Many a buckler beaming bright,
Many a green marlote is spied,
Many a ren aljube beside,
Many a plume of gallant air,
Many a rich-grain'd cappellare,
Many a boot a-borzegui,
Many a silken string and tie,
Many a spur of gold there clung,
Many a silver stirrup swung.
All the men that rode that day
Were expert at battle-fray:
Midst of all that pomp and pow'r
Chyquo Monarch of the Moor.
Moorish dames and maidens high
Them from proud Alhambra eye;
And the Moorish Queen so grey
In this guise was heard to say:
„Speed thee hence my son and love!
Mahomet thy Guardian prove!
Crown'd with honor back from Jaen
May he bring thee soon again."

THE FORSAKEN.

From the Spanish.

Up I rose, O mother, early
On the blest Saint Juan's morn;
By the sea I saw a damsel,
Saw a damsel all forlorn.

Lonely there she wash'd her garments
And upon a rose-tree hung;
Whilst the garments there were drying
She a plaintiff ditty sung.

,,O my love, my fickle lover—
Where to find him shall I stray?"
Up and down the strand she hurried
Singing, singing this sad lay.

In her hand a comb she carried,
All of gold, to comb her hair;
,,Tell me, tell me, gentle sailor—
Heaven take thee 'neath it's care—
Hast thou seen my fickle lover,
Hast thou seen him any where?"

STANZAS.

From the Portuguese.

A fool is he who in the lap
Basking of every smiling joy,
Will each and all with fear alloy
Of what some future day may hap.

Let him enjoy his present state;
For he but double make his woes,
Who midst the future's shadows goes
To meet the ills of murky fate.

MY EIGHTEENTH YEAR.

From the French.

Where is my eighteenth year? far back
Upon life's variegated track;
Yet fondly oft I turn my eye,
And for my eighteenth year I sigh.

Each pleasure then I took with zest,
And hope was inmate of my breast—
Enchanting hope, consoling thing,
The plucker out of sorrow's sting.

The sun above shone brighter then,
Fairer were women, kinder men;
If tears I shed, they soon were o'er,
And I was happier than before.

The minstrel-wight of ancient day
Wish'd that the twelve months all were May;
I wish that every year I see
The eighteenth of my life could be.

SONG.

From the Rommany or Gypsy Language

The strength of the ox,
The wit of the fox,
And the leveret's speed,—
Full oft, to oppose
To their numerous foes,
The Rommany need.

Our horses they take,
Our waggons they break,
And ourselves they seize,
In their prisons to coop,
Where we pine and droop,
For want of breeze.

When the dead swallow
The fly shall follow
O'ēr Burra-panee,
Then we will forget
The wrongs we have met,
And forgiving be.

THE END.

THE
𝔗alisman.

FROM THE RUSSIAN

OF

ALEXANDER PUSHKIN.

With other Pieces.

St. Petersburg.
Printed by Schulz and Beneze.
1835.

THE TALISMAN.

From the Russian of Pushkin.

Where fierce the surge with awful bellow
Doth ever lash the rocky wall;
And where the moon most brightly mellow
Dost beam when mists of evening fall;
Where midst his harem's countless blisses
The Moslem spends his vital span;
A Sorceress there with gentle kisses
Presented me a Talisman.

And said: until thy latest minute
Preserve, preserve my Talisman;
A secret power it holds within it—
'Twas love, true love the gift did plan.
From pest on land, or death on ocean,
When hurricanes its surface fan,
O object of my fond devotion!
Thou scap'st not by my Talisman.

The gem in Eastern mine which slumbers,
Or ruddy gold 'twill not bestow;
'Twill not subdue the turban'd numbers,
Before the Prophet's shrine which bow;
Nor high through air on friendly pinions

Can bear thee swift to home and clan,
From mournful climes and strange dominions-
From South to North—my Talisman.

But oh! when crafty eyes thy reason
With sorceries sudden seek to move,
And when in Night's mysterious season
Lips cling to thine, but not in love—
From proving then, dear youth, a booty
To those who falsely would trepan
From new heart wounds, and lapse from duty,
Protect thee shall my Talisman.

THE MERMAID.

From the Russian of Pushkin.

Close by a lake, begirt with forest,
To save his soul, a Monk intent,
In fasting, prayer and labours sorest
His days and nights, secluded, spent;
A grave already to receive him
He fashion'd, stooping, with his spade,
And speedy, speedy death to give him,
Was all that of the Saints he pray'd.

As once in summer's time of beauty,
On bended knee, before his door,
To God he paid his fervent duty,
The woods grew more and more obscure:
Down o'er the lake a fog descended,
And slow the full moon, red as blood,
Midst threat'ning clouds up heaven wended—
Then gazed the Monk upon the flood.

He gaz'd, and, fear his mind surprising,
Himself no more the hermit knows:
He sees with foam the waters rising,
And then subsiding to repose,

And sudden, light as night-ghost wanders,
A female thence her form uprais'd,
Pale as the snow which winter squanders,
And on the bank herself she plac'd.

She gazes on the hermit hoary,
And combs her long hair, tress by tress;
The Monk he quakes, but on the glory
Looks wistful of her loveliness;
Now becks with hand that winsome creature
And now she noddeth with her head,
Then sudden, like a fallen meteor,
She plunges in her watery bed.

No sleep that night the old man cheereth,
No prayer throughout next day he pray'd
Still, still, against his wish, appeareth
Before him that mysterious maid.
Darkness again the wood investeth,
The moon midst clouds is seen to sail,
And once more on the margin resteth
The maiden beautiful and pale.

With head she bow'd, with look she courted
And kiss'd her hand repeatedly,
Splashed with the water, gaily sported,
And wept and laugh'd like infancy—

She names the monk, with tones heart-urging
Exclaims ,,O Monk, come, come to me!"
Then sudden midst the waters merging
All, all is in tranquillity.

On the third night the hermit fated
Beside those shores of sorcery,
Sat and the damsel fair awaited,
And dark the woods began to be—
The beams of morn the night mists scatter,
No Monk is seen then, well a day!
And only, only in the water
The lasses view'd his beard of grey.

ANCIENT RUSSIAN SONG.

i.

The windel-straw nor grass so shook and trembled;
As the good and gallant stripling shook and trembled;
A linen shirt so fine his frame invested,
O'er the shirt was drawn a bright pelisse of scarlet
The sleeves of that pelisse depended backward,
The lappets of its front were button'd backward,
And were spotted with the blood of unbelievers;
See the good and gallant stripling reeling goeth,
From his eyeballs hot and briny tears distilling;
On his bended bow his figure he supporteth,
Till his bended bow has lost its goodly gilding;
Not a single soul the stripling good encounter'd,
Till encounter'd he the mother dear who bore him:
O my boy, O my treasure, and my darling!
By what mean hast thou render'd thee so drunken,
To the clay that thou bowest down thy figure,
And the grass and the windel-straws art grasping?
To his Mother thus the gallant youth made answer:
'Twas not I, O mother dear, who made me drunken,
But the Sultan of the Turks has made me drunken
With three potent, various potations;
The first of them his keenly cutting sabre;
The next of them his never failing jav'lin;
The third of them his pistol's leaden bullet.

ii.

O rustle not, ye verdant oaken branches!
Whilst I tell the gallant stripling's tale of daring;
When this morn they led the gallant youth to judgment
Before the dread tribunal of the grand Tsar,
Then our Tsar and Gosudar began to question:
Tell me, tell me, little lad, and peasant bantling!
Who assisted thee to ravage and to plunder;
I trow thou hadst full many wicked comrades.
I'll tell thee, Tsar! our country's hope and glory,
I'll tell thee all the truth, without a falsehood:
Thou must know that I had comrades, four in number;
Of my comrades four the first was gloomy midnight;
The second was a steely dudgeon dagger;
The third it was a swift and speedy courser;
The fourth of my companions was a bent bow;
My messengers were furnace-harden'd arrows.
Replied the Tsar, our country's hope and glory:
Of a truth, thou little lad, and peasant's bantling!
In thieving thou art skill'd and giving answers;
For thy answers and thy thieving I'll reward thee
With a house upon the windy plain constructed
Of two pillars high, surmounted by a cross-beam.

iii.

O thou field of my delight so fair and verdant!
Thou scene of all my happiness and pleasure!
O how charmingly Nature hath array'd thee
With the soft green grass and juicy clover,
And with corn-flowers blooming and luxuriant.
One thing there is alone, that doth deform thee;
In the midst of thee, O field, so fair and verdant!
A clump of bushes stands—a clump of hazels,
Upon their very top there sits an eagle,
And upon the bushes' top—upon the hazels,
Compress'd within his claw he holds a raven,
And its hot blood he sprinkles on the dry ground;
And beneath the bushes' clump—beneath the hazels,
Lies void of life the good and gallant stripling;
All wounded. pierc'd and mangled is his body.
As the little tiny swallow or the chaffinch,
Round their warm and cosey nest are seen to hover,
So hovers there the mother dear who bore him;
And aye she weeps, as flows a river's water;
His sister weeps as flows a streamlet's water;
His youthful wife, as falls the dew from heaven—
The Sun, arising, dries the dew of heaven.

ANCIENT BALLAD.

From the Malo Russian.

From the wood a sound is gliding,
Vapours dense the plain are hiding,
How yon Dame her son is chiding.
„Son, away! nor longer tarry!
Would the Turks thee off would carry!"
„Ha; the Turkmen know and heed me;
Coursers good the Turkmen breed me."

From the wood a sound is gliding,
Vapours dense the plain are hiding,
Still that Dame her son is chiding:
„Hence, begone! nor longer tarry!
Would the Horde (*) thee off would carry!"
„Ha! the Horde has learnt to prize me;
„'Tis the Horde with gold supplies me."

Brings his horse his eldest sister,
And the next his arms, which glister,
Whilst the third, with childish prattle,
Cries, „when wilt return from battle?"

(*) The Tartar Horde,—generally known by the appellation of „The Golden," which, some centuries since, was the dreaded and terrible scourge of Southern Russia.

„ Fill thy hand with sands, my blossom!
Sow them on the rock's rude bosom,
Night and morning stroll to view them,
With thy briny tears bedew them,
And when they shall sprout in glory
I'll return me from the foray."

From the wood a sound is gliding,
Vapours dense the plain are hiding,
Cries the Dame in anxious measure:
„ Stay, I'll wash thy head, my treasure!"
„ Me shall wash the rains which splash me,
Me shall comb the thorns which gash me,
Me shall dry the winds which lash me."

THE RENEGADE.

From the Polish of Mickiewicz.

Now pay ye the heed that is fitting,
Whilst I sing ye the Iran adventure;
The Pasha on sofa was sitting
In his harem's glorious centre.

Greek sang and Tcherkass for his pleasure,
And Kergeesian captive is dancing;
In the eyes of the first heaven's azure,
And in those black of Eblis is glancing.

But the Pasha's attention is failing,
O'er his visage his fair turban stealeth;
From tchebouk (*) he sleep is inhaling
Whilst round him sweet vapours he dealeth.

What rumour without is there breeding?
Ye fair ranks asunder why wend ye?
Kyslar Aga (**), a strange captive leading,
Cometh forward and crieth. „Efendy!

Whose face has the power when present
Midst the stars in divan which do muster,

(*) Turkish pipe.
(**) Keeper of the women.

Which amidst the gems of night's crescent
Has the blaze of Aldeboran's lustre.

Glance nearer, bright star! I have tiding,
Glad tiding, behold how in duty
From far Lehistan the wind, gliding.
Has brought this fresh tribute of beauty.

In the Padishaw's garden there bloometh,
In proud Istambul, no such blossom;
From the wintry regions she cometh
Whose memory so lives in thy bosom."

Then the gauzes removes he which shade her,
At her beauty all wonder intensely;
One moment the Pasha survey'd her,
And, dropping his tchebouk, without sense lay

His turban has fallen from his forehead,
To assist him the bystanders started—
His mouth foams, his face blackens horrid—
See the Renegade's soul has departed.

www.ingramcontent.com/pod-product-compliance
Lightning Source LLC
Chambersburg PA
CBHW020113170426
43199CB00009B/514